love

remains

true

written and illustrated by
corin filmer

i

acknowledgments

my heart is filled with gratitude.

alan, my husband, for all his love and
encouragement, plus best tech support
ever

eliane, chloe and ryan, my children who
help with social media ideas,
marketing, and cheer me on

klaus, my dear friend who has always
encouraged me to share my poems and
publish a second book

sheri cleary who continues to challenge
and inspire my growth

the wwtw sisters who are amazing
sisters in Christ

martha sandino for her imagination,
wisdom, encouragement, and prayers

connie johnson for graciously proof
reading my book again

most importantly God, because He is so
faithful and does not give up on me

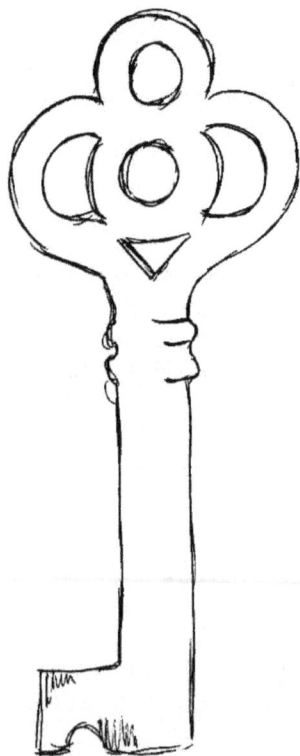

"trust the Lord with all your heart and lean not on your own understanding"
Proverbs 3: 5-6

about "loved loving love[1]"

no book launch celebration.
no women's gathering to share my poetry
and encourage each other's hearts.

just a world closing down in fear.

God's timing is perfect, often repeated
in my mind. all i could do was to
trust, give it to God, and see what He
would do.

so many trust-building moments:

books began to sell on Amazon. books
were given to people and organizations,
as I felt led. people wrote some
beautiful reviews (each one blessed me
more than they will ever know). phone
calls with kind words of favorite poems
that had touched hearts, often received
just when i was questioning what in the
world i was doing. one beautiful moment
of an outdoor book-signing in october
in the middle of a pandemic! books were
ordered, flyers made, thoughts and
plans were shared on social media.
would anyone come? tears rolled down
mask-covered faces, as friends came,
prayed, supported, and saw each other
for the first time in months.
such joy in reunion.

i know God has many more trust-building
moments ahead of me. all in His perfect
timing.

---

[1] loved loving love is my first poetry book

contents

know You more

You quench my thirst
You feed my soul
You're all that i need
all that i need
to define me

Your love calls me
and shows me
the way

as i take a breath
and feel You close
You're all i need
all i need
to define me

Your love helps me
know you more

turn to Me

turn to Me
when your heart is broken
turn to Me
when the pain won't go

give to Me
your fears and failures
turn to Me
let your tears flow

as they fall
so My love in you
grows deeper

and so

again and again
turn to Me

united in love

happy eyes
outstretched hands
open hearts
joy in the reunion

old friends
new stories
peace in each other's arms

differences melt
in songs and laughter
working side by side
towards a better life
sharing together

united in love

14

imperfect hearts

we bring our hearts ...
imperfect
as they are

scars deep within
hidden so well
even from ourselves

tarnished
            by words
            by deeds
            by life

You welcome
each one

as we bring it to the cross
    where love heals
and offer up each pain
    and let go
    one by one
as our trust deepens
    and love remains true

hope

hope
a living
certain
absolute
hope

in our hearts
our minds
our lives

a place
to rest
        safe secure
to abide
        in His blessing
to grow
        in His knowledge
to be filled
        with joy and peace
to share
        a glimpse of eternity
        to a broken world

hope
a living
certain
absolute
hope

we give our hearts
        our minds
        our lives

to Him

in the shadow of the cross

in the shadow of the cross
Your sacrifice
Your blood
flowed
for me

i am left
in tears
helpless
convicted

by man's brutality
God's love
my guilt
and an invitation
to sit at Your feet
as i am

in awe of Your love
thankful for Your mercy
desperate for Your grace

yield

nourish me
speak to me
show me
let me feel
Your love

let me open
to the warmth
of Your light
willingly
letting go
        my fears
        my doubts
        my independence

and accept
the gift
of
who i am
in You

the nail

hard and cold
sharpened to a point
grey
stark
cold

nothing to please the eye
or offer hope
to a searching heart

yet beauty lies
in the strong lines
and symmetry

take my pride
take my lies
take my selfish
          hardened heart

and blow by blow
          blow by bloody blow

nail them to the cross

Holy Spirit

Your spirit calls to know me
to breathe life
where darkness only reigned

to bring power
  change the hardest heart
    and make beauty
      from the pieces that remain

to lift my prayers
on clouds of incense to the heavens
to transform lives
and love beyond my gain

to show
the path for each and every footstep
to fill me
with the purest burning flame

so others get to taste the sweetest joy
that even in their pain
You love them

Your spirit calls to know me
and mine yearns to know You more

gratitude

i am broken
weeping at Your feet

let my tears fall shamelessly
as a never ending offering of gratitude
from a heart
        so desperate for forgiveness
        so humbled by my need

let my tears be tears of praise
that spring
from my endless thankfulness

let my tears lavishly worship You
as i see the depth of Your forgiveness
in Your unending love

amazed

amazed at Your love
that You would care
that You would even know my name

who am i to You?
insignificant
in a world
where my worth is small?

yet
    You chose me
    You chose to value me

to raise me up
to a place i don't deserve

and in return
    in Your love
    i am complete

in humility

in humility
i come to You
my eyes turned
from distraction
to focus on You

where i am satisfied
as this moment
lost in You
lasts forever

i am sorry ...

i am sorry for ...

taking You for granted
denying Your existence
turning from You
ignoring Your wisdom
rejecting Your love
stealing Your glory
questioning Your truth
refusing to listen
missing Your beauty
forgetting Your presence
neglecting our relationship
overlooking my need for You
focusing on me
disobeying You
disregarding Your involvement
scorning Your design
not heeding Your words
not being thankful

and all the other ways
i am not even aware of ...

Emmanuel

a star proclaims
the heavens rejoice
the birth

so wondrous yet so meek
can it be?

the Maker of the universe
would choose poverty and dirt
to crown His own?

would choose humanity
with whom to dwell?

would choose a helpless babe
to share life's joys and pain?

to see the best and know our worst
and love us all the same?

would choose a sinner's death
to bring the hope of heaven
in His name?

a star proclaims
the heavens rejoice
so we may do the same

the throne

come to the throne
an invitation
for us all

draw near
bring your doubt
  and find understanding
bring your insecurity
  and find trust
bring your fear
  and find mercy
bring your weakness
  and find strength

find peace in your heart
and know
    that
        He knows
        He feels
        He cares

and only He can fill our hearts with
truth

come near
in prayer
open your heart
with praise
again and again
whisper His name
abide in His love
and find rest

in your need

bring Me your heart
your pain
share the loneliness
the empty days
rest in your need
your need of Me

trust Me

when you show me the scars
I receive each one
as a gift
to treasure
each tear brings us closer

your need
in My abundance
My love
in your heart

stand

Your love
a love
  so pure
    so beautiful
  endless
free

to be
  Yours
to shine
  into lives
to melt
  hearts
to finally know peace
to be
  seen
and stand
in
Your love

empty days

empty days
filled with fear and doubt
uncertainty
too much
and not enough

old habits die hard
leaving new normals
my heart aches
for the suffering

missing
family, friends, community
so alone
inaction
breeds despair

how long?

show me Your beauty
Your steadfast love
be the song in my heart
whisper my name
let me see You
in the sunrise
hear You
in the breeze
remind me of Your faithfulness
renew my mind
wake me from my slumber
be my hope
heal my heart
take my hand
and lead me

in a new place

leaving the old
        the fear
        the "not enough" voices

bringing the jagged edges
of unforgiving words
and broken deeds

drawing near

near
enough
to hear
You call
a new name

near
enough
to be still
in a new place

near
enough
to dwell
with the most High

prayer

oh hear my heart
my praise
open my mind
to Your wonders
and mysteries

as i sing
of my love
let my words
reach You

as we share
precious moments
together
and Your words
reach out
to my heart
and Your spirit reveals
truth
to mine

together

here we stand
together
in a synergy
of love

in our humility
we move
with a desire
        buried
        inside
awakened
        for a purpose
and used
        in quiet confidence

to work
        in lives
to share
        gifts
to reach
        needs
to reflect
        love
to show
        Your glory

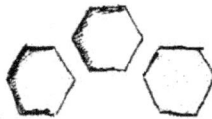

creation calls

a silent symphony of beauty
my senses bathed
in awe

my heart
my mind
my spirit

reach to grasp
heaven's song
Your masterpiece
endless wonder
calls to me
in hushed whisper

hear Me
see Me
know Me

all that i need

when all i feel
is a weakness within
an empty void
hidden
and dark

when i've tried all i can
to fill it myself
but nothing succeeds ...

love does

love does
    with a power
love does
    with such strength
love does
    in perfection
love does
    never spent
love does
    with a beauty
love does
    in true joy
love does
    in obedience
        patience
            and grace

love takes my weakness
    my sin and my need
love lights the darkness
    fills the void
      is all
        that i need

take it all

Your will be done

in my heart
in my life
in my weakness
in my fear
in my need
in my tears

here I am
on my knees

take it all

in Your wisdom
in Your grace
in Your mercy
in Your blood
in Your name
in Your love

faith

close your eyes
open hands
and hearts
receive
the gift

sit with
look at
hear Me

just us

learn to know
    My voice
    My plans
    My desires

abandon yourself
and trust

step out
in spirit

focus
on our time
together

My promise
and your obedience

I will speak
and you will follow

thankfulness

i sit
and ponder
my heart full
of gratitude
undeserving
as i am

You love me

immersed in Your spirit
i can

    show compassion
    speak kindly
    live humbly
    learn meekness
    find hope
    wait patiently
    abide

in the fullness of Your heart

in the storm
there is joy

with You
in Your presence

in my heart
    in time spent
        delighting
in You
  in Your words
    in Your love

there is peace
with You

in surrendering
  my mind
    in prayer
      with You

in gratitude
  in praise
    abiding

with You
in control

there is joy
in the storm

five days

five days
just five days
for human hearts
to shift

from palms to thorns
    cheers to curses
    praise to pariah
    King to criminal

only five days

fickle hearts
    despised Him
    disgraced Him
    rejected Him

Heaven witnessed
    power in submission
    strength in obedience
    blessings in scorn
    healing in wounds
    love in enmity
    forgiveness in sacrifice
    redemption from sin

for me

The King bowed
for me

humbled
clothed
in servitude
washed my feet
washed the dirt
from
my life

pouring out
His own
on the cross

loving me
to the limit
His blood opened
The Kingdom
made the way
into peace
        life
          eternity

for me
The King bowed

giving

i sit
a heart full
from giving

so blessed
to share
        time
        words
        prayers
        food
        lives

to feel
Your presence
in our needs

we bless
yet
are blessed
    much more

let our hands
and voices lift

a heart full
from
Your infinite giving

tears

weeping again
but now
tears of rejoicing

You see me
and bring to mind
the first time
together
those tears
of desperation
  alone
    hopeless

now i sing
hands raised
to You
in awe

what transformation
as Your love
fills
the emptiness

i am
before you
  so thankful
    so needy
      so blessed

quicken my heart
  my soul
    my life
      is Yours

                    the key

    i close my eyes
    and see
    more clearly
    than i have for years

    this key
    more ancient than the heavens
    calls my name
    as it has always done

    only now
    do i reach to touch
    its perfect trinity

    come open me

about you

you are living through very uncertain
days. there is little in your life that
seems steady or reliable. events are
happening every day that can make you
lie awake at night worrying about your
future. nevertheless, there is one
thing that is unchanging that you can
put your trust in.

God loves you and wants a relationship
with you.

He revealed himself to me one day as i
sat weeping on the floor of a hotel
bathroom, unable to go on in my own
strength any more. i had ignored Him
for years, lived my own life, trusted
in my own abilities. He met me with
love, kindness, forgiveness, and joy.
like a father welcoming a lost child
home. my heart responded and I needed
to get to know Him more. that led me to
asking a lot of questions, visiting a
church, joining a bible study, and
ultimately writing the poem "the key."

His call for a relationship with you is
getting more and more compelling. can
you sense the urgency?

investigate this life-changing
relationship while you still can. don't
keep putting Him off.

take time with each poem. sit with it
awhile. pray about it and journal your
thoughts. write scriptures that come to
mind or draw your response. be still and
let His creativity come through you.
share poems that resonate with you.

connect with me and share your thoughts,
your favorite poem, your journaling,
your heart via:

website corinfilmer.com

Instagram @corinwrites

corin@corinfilmer.com

"He wants not only us
but *everyone* saved, you know,
everyone to get to know the
truth *we've* learned: that there's one
God and only one, and one Priest-
Mediator between God and us—Jesus, who
offered himself in exchange for
everyone held captive by sin, to set
them all free. Eventually the news is
going to get out. This and this only
has been my appointed work: getting
this news to those who have never heard
of God, and explaining how it works by
simple faith and plain truth."

1 Timothy 2-3-7   (the message version
of the Bible)

www.ingramcontent.com/pod-product-compliance
Lightning Source LLC
Chambersburg PA
CBHW021142020426
42331CB00005B/864